baby
animals

baby
animals

by William Lach

THE METROPOLITAN MUSEUM OF ART

ABRAMS BOOKS FOR YOUNG READERS
New York

baby
dogs

Baby dogs are called puppies.

baby
cats

Tigers are big cats, and their babies are called cubs.

baby
goats

Baby goats are called kids!

baby
bats

Baby bats are called pups.

baby
boy

Little boys are also baby animals!

baby
bear

Baby bears are also called cubs.

baby
who

Baby owls are called owlets.

baby
where

Baby elephants are called calves.

baby
girl

Little girls are also baby animals!

baby
deer

Baby deer are called fawns.

baby
soon

Baby birds hatch from eggs.

baby
here

Baby chickens are called chicks.

baby
pinch

Baby crayfish are called hatchlings.

baby
prickle

Baby porcupines are called porcupettes.

baby
bounce

Baby kangaroos are called joeys.

baby
tickle

Baby monkeys are called babies!

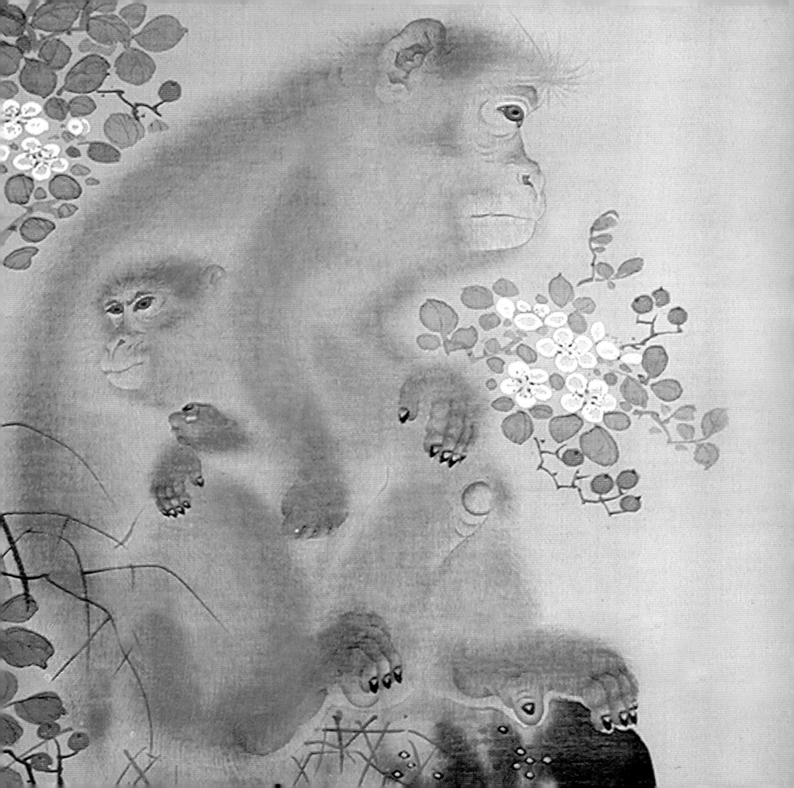

baby
cow

Baby cows are also called calves.

baby
sheep

Baby sheep are called lambs.

baby
meow

Baby cats are called kittens.

baby
sleep

Baby boars are called piglets.

Except where noted, the works of art in this book are in the collection of The Metropolitan Museum of Art.

BABY DOGS
Embroidered Carpet
Zeruah Higley Guernsey Caswell, American
(Vermont), 1805–ca. 1895
Wool, embroidered in chain-stitch,
13 ft. 4 in. x 12 ft. 3 in., ca. 1832–35
Gift of Katharine Keyes, in memory of her
father, Homer Eaton Keyes, 1938 38.157

BABY CATS
Tiger and Cubs
Jean-Léon Gérôme, French, 1824–1904
Oil on canvas, 29 x 36 in., ca. 1884
Bequest of Susan P. Colgate, in memory of her
husband, Romulus R. Colgate, 1936 36.162.4

BABY GOATS
Study for Three Kids Before a Fence
Parmigianino (Giralamo
Francesco Maria Mazzola), Italian
(Parma), 1503–1540
Pen and bistre on paper,
5⅞ x 3¾ in., after 1530
MUSÉE CONDÉ, Chantilly, France
Courtesy Giraudon, the Bridgeman
Art Library

BABY BATS
Dragon Robe
Chinese, Qing dynasty (1644–1911)
Silk gauze embroidered with silk
and metallic thread, 56 x 53½ in.,
late 18th century
Purchase, Joseph Pulitzer Bequest,
1935 35.84.8

BABY BOY
The First Babe
Jehan Georges Vibert, French, 1840–1902
Watercolor on paper, 14 ¹¹⁄₁₆ x 17 ¾ in., 1872
Catharine Lorillard Wolfe Collection,
Bequest of Catharine Lorillard Wolfe, 1887
87.15.8

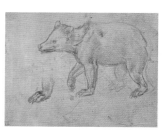

BABY BEAR
A Bear Walking
Leonardo da Vinci, Italian (Florentine),
1452–1519
Metalpoint on light buff prepared paper,
4¹⁄₁₆ x 5¼ in., ca. 1490
Robert Lehman Collection, 1975
1975.1.369

BABY WHO
Little Screech Owl
John J. Bowen, American,
ca. 1801–?1856, lithographer
After John James Audubon,
American, 1785–1851
Hand-colored lithograph,
10 ¼ x 6 ¼ in., 1840–44
Gift of Mrs. Darwin S. Morse,
1963 63.709.5(1), pl. 40

BABY WHERE
Allaitement du petit éléphant
J. P. L. L. Houel, French, 1735–1813
Histoire naturelle des deux éléphans . . ., pl. 18
Etching with engraving, 7 ⅜ x 9 ½ in., 1803
The Elisha Whittelsey Collection, The Elisha
Whittelsey Fund, 1953 53.554.5

BABY GIRL
Feeding the Ducks
Mary Cassatt, American, 1845–1926
Drypoint and aquatint printed in color,
11 ½ x 15 ¾ in., ca. 1894
H. O. Havemeyer Collection, Bequest of Mrs.
H. O. Havemeyer, 1929 29.107.100

BABY DEER
Doe and Two Fawns
Arthur Fitzwilliam Tait, American, 1819–1905
Oil on academy board, 10 x 14 in., 1882
Gift of Mrs. Darwin S. Morse, 1963
63.200.7

BABY SOON
Flowers by a Stone Vase
Peter Faes, Flemish, 1750–1814
Oil on wood, 20 x 14 ⅛ in., 1786
Bequest of Catherine D. Wentworth,
1948 48.187.737

BABY HERE
Album Leaf: Young Bird with Flowers
Watanabe Seitei, Japanese, 1851–1918
Ink and color on silk, 14 x 10 ⅝ in.
Charles Stewart Smith Collection,
Gift of Mrs. Charles Stewart Smith,
Charles Stewart Smith, Jr., and
Howard Caswell Smith, in memory
of Charles Stewart Smith, 1914
14.76.61.53

BABY PINCH
Album Leaf: Shellfish (detail)
Watanabe Seitei, Japanese,
1851–1918
Ink and color on silk, 14 ¼ x 10 ⅞ in.
Charles Stewart Smith Collection,
Gift of Mrs. Charles Stewart
Smith, Charles Stewart Smith, Jr.,
and Howard Caswell Smith, in
memory of Charles Stewart Smith,
1914 14.76.61.37

BABY PRICKLE
Porcupine
German school, 1890
Plate from *Brehms Tierleben . . .*, vol. 2, p. 560
Colored lithograph, 4 ⅞ x 7 ⅝ in.
PRIVATE COLLECTION
Courtesy the Bridgeman Art Library

BABY BOUNCE
Bark Painting
Australia (Western Arnhem
Land), early to mid-20th century
Bark, paint, H. 40 ½ in.
The Michael C. Rockefeller
Memorial Collection, Bequest
of Nelson A. Rockefeller, 1979
1979.206.1514

BABY TICKLE
Monkey with Baby and Autumn Flowers
Attributed to the school of Mori Sosen,
Japanese, 1747–1821
Scroll painting, ink and colors on paper, after 1800
PACIFIC ASIA MUSEUM, Pasadena
Gift of Dr. George W. Housner, 2001.21.81

BABY COW
Weaning the Calves
Rosa Bonheur, French, 1822–1899
Oil on canvas, 25 ⅝ x 32 in., 1879
Catharine Lorillard Wolfe Collection,
Bequest of Catharine Lorillard Wolfe, 1887
87.15.109

BABY SHEEP
Springtime
Charles-Émile Jacque, French,
1813–1894
Oil on wood, 16 x 11 ½ in.
Bequest of Lillian S. Timken,
1959 60.71.10

BABY MEOW
Pussy's Return
Currier and Ives, publishers, American, active
1857–1907
Hand-colored lithograph, 8½ x 12½ in.
Bequest of Adele S. Colgate, 1962 63.550.314

BABY SLEEP
Netsuke: Boar
Japanese, 18th century
Ivory, L. 2¼ in.
Bequest of Stephen Whitney Phoenix, 1881
81.1.91

Except where noted, the works of art in this book are in the collection of The Metropolitan Museum of Art.

FRONT COVER: *Embroidered Carpet* (detail). Zeruah Higley Guernsey Caswell, American (Vermont), 1805–ca. 1895. Wool, embroidered in chain-stitch, 13 ft. 4 in. x 12 ft. 3 in., ca. 1832–35. Gift of Katharine Keyes, in memory of her father, Homer Eaton Keyes, 1938 38.157

ENDPAPER DESIGN: *Stencil with Autumn Grasses* (detail). Japanese, 19th century. Paper reinforced with silk, 17½ x 16 in. Gift of Clarence McK. Lewis, 1953 53.101.60

TITLE PAGE: *Doe and Two Fawns* (detail). Arthur Fitzwilliam Tait, American, 1819–1905. Oil on academy board, 10 x 14 in., 1882. Gift of Mrs. Darwin S. Morse, 1963 63.200.7

BACK COVER: *Album Leaf: Young Bird with Flowers* (detail). Watanabe Seitei, Japanese, 1851–1918. Ink and color on silk, 14 x 10⅝ in. Charles Stewart Smith Collection, Gift of Mrs. Charles Stewart Smith, Charles Stewart Smith, Jr., and Howard Caswell Smith, in memory of Charles Stewart Smith, 1914 14.76.61.53

Published by The Metropolitan Museum of Art, New York, and Harry N. Abrams, Inc.,
New York

First Edition
Printed in China
11 10 09 08 07   10 9 8 7 6 5 4 3 2 1

Produced by the Department of Special Publications, The Metropolitan Museum of Art: Robie Rogge, Publishing Manager; William Lach, Senior Editor; Anna Raff, Designer; Mahin Kooros, Production Editor.

Photography of works from The Metropolitan Museum of Art is by The Metropolitan Museum of Art Photograph Studio.

Visit the Museum's Web site: www.metmuseum.org

Library of Congress Cataloging-in-Publication Data:

Lach, William, 1968-
  Baby animals / by William Lach.
    p. cm.

  ISBN-13 (MMA): 978-1-58839-182-7 (hardcover with jacket)
  ISBN-10 (MMA): 1-58839-182-5 (hardcover with jacket)
  ISBN-13 (Abrams): 978-0-8109-9457-7 (hardcover with jacket)
  ISBN-10 (Abrams): 0-8109-9457-7 (hardcover with jacket)

  1. Animals—Infancy—Juvenile literature. I. Title.

  QL763.L334 2008
  591.3'9—dc22

                    2007003856

HNA
harry n. abrams, inc.
a subsidiary of La Martinière Groupe
115 West 18th Street
New York, NY 10011
www.hnabooks.com